MW01223334

We Called It "The Country"
and other poems

by Lucia Blinn

We Called It "The Country"
And Other Poems by Lucia Blinn

© 2011 Lucia Blinn
All Rights Reserved
ISBN# 978-0-9763675-3-6

18 17 16 15 14   4 5

Published by First Flight Books
A division of Bruce Bendinger Creative Communications, Inc.
2144 N. Hudson • Chicago, IL 60614
773-871-1179 • FX 773-281-4643
www.firstflightbooks.com

FIRST FLIGHT BOOKS

Book Design: Meredith Raub
Cover Design: Gregory S. Paus

For further information, you may e-mail the author:
luciablinn@gmail.com

For my mother
who read my future in an 8th grade term paper

How do you know when a poem is finished?
Gwendolyn Brooks said that you never know.
At some point, you just abandon it.

Herewith, the abandoned, beginning with a new arrival,
traversing various cities and states of mind,
and ending away from the fray in the country.
The secret, say the sages, is to live close to nature.

Contents

Tina

I was three-and-a-half the day The Baby came home
to make us an even four girls and four boys.
Isn't she a cute little monkey? Mom asked,
everyone peering into the bassinet at the tiny
black-haired infant. *Hi, little monkey,* I said.
No! Don't you call her that! Mom scolded.
And there it was, the first bruising humiliation.
Oblivious, she turned to naming the non-simian.
Kristina, suggested older sister, Martha.
How about Crystal? I piped up, anxious to regain
approval or perhaps already rewriting.
My contribution ignored, Kristina it was.

The beautiful green-eyed babe affected me
not at all except for the morning she was sunning
in her ivory wicker pram and a visitor exclaimed:
Isn't she pretty! Seeing me pathetic with pain,
she added, *Oh, you're cute, too.* That did it.
At four, I knew looks wouldn't work;
I'd have to crank up some talent.

Hoisted on a bench at family parties, I regaled them
with reedy renditions of love songs Martha played
on the piano. *Ah, Sweet Mystery of Life. One Kiss.*
When Day is Done. At eight, I branched into hairdressing.
Cousins Sally, Mildred and Sophie sat patiently
at their mother's oil cloth-covered kitchen table
while I brushed and bobby-pinned them into heady
new looks. At ten, I was producing, directing
and starring in living room theatricals. Multi-tasking,
I was also performing stunts for a friend's swing shows.
No athlete I, my feats were less than stunning.

At nineteen, having fizzled at school, there was nothing
left but Advertising, a stony road of minor wins, many losses
and addictive paychecks, a thirty-year slog that finally
sputtered away. Today, the pretty baby lives happily ever
after and big sister continues to produce and parade
her wares. *Wanna hear a poem?*

December 7, 1941

December 7, 1941

I was five-years-old on the day
something jarred me away from my play.
Mom was upset in a terrible way.
But I pictured it shiny and beautiful.
How could a Pearl Harbor be bad?

June 6, 1944

Great excitement around the radio.
Something about The War.
It's D Day, Mom said.
*You'll never forget this happened
on your birthday.*

It was one of our favorite games.
As Anns, Tina and I were moms who cared
for our dolls and lived in adjacent houses:
the steps to the second floor.
Janes were career girls who went to an office
by way of getting into the tub and pulling the shower
curtain/elevator door. Our desk was the tiny telephone
table in the living room. Work consisted of organizing
pieces of paper, sharpening and arranging pencils
and making and taking phantom phone calls.
At any point, one of us started a frantic recitation
that began: *I've got...*instantly prompting the other in a race
to finish with: *the whole wide world full of beautiful things.*
Whoever got the words out first won the priceless prize
leaving the other bereft.

Memory playing its own game, Tina will tell you
that Janes stayed home and Anns went to work.
Never mind, it was fortune-telling all the same.
We each grew up as both. Tina worked in a school
and I in an office where I wrote on paper and made
phone calls. And we minded our babies, albeit in houses
rather more than two steps apart.

Closet Math

The occupants in that two-story house
included parents in one bedroom,
a younger sister and I in another,
and at one time, two brothers home
from the war in the third.
When an older sister and her husband
slept there, I was humiliated trying to peek
through the keyhole.

The bedrooms were small, closets minute.
We didn't collect clothes then.
No multiple skirts, no stacks of sweaters.
There was just what we needed
for school and play and church.
Mom and her sister sewed much of that.
Definitely un-needed was the black lacy
dancing affair financed with babysitting funds.
Anyone resembling a partner danced
only in my dreams.

Mother Teresa had the clothes on her back,
one set in the laundry, one in the closet.
So did the nuns who taught us.
I continue as their student now, having come
full circle from the bare bones of that first tiny closet
to the long parade of designer designs I couldn't dress
without to the give-me-this-day-my-daily jeans
and tees, otherwise known as freedom.

School Supplies

What promise, what power in those words.
And in the crisp autumn sound of *September.*
That was the year's real beginning.
The burnished days when the last bits of summer
blew away. We raked crunchy leaves into piles,
lit smoky bonfires and inhaled the now-forbidden
scent that signaled sweaters. Mom supervised
the boys in the annual washing of the storm windows;
the kitchen radio turned way up with the Tigers
winding down the season. In the pre-TV forties,
there was still quiet in our heads for dreaming;
time enough for reading under a tree.
We got ready for school with new shoes
and plaid skirts and *school supplies*—fresh new pencils
and tablets that teased you into expectations of A's
but rarely mid-wifed more than a B.

Suddenly, it was a different September,
a different school, all-girls Dominican High.
Tables in the basement of this strange
grand place held stacks of hefty textbooks.
Costly clean-smelling new ones and volumes
already used that I would use as well.
Across the way, nuns were selling uniforms:
a straight skirt and short-sleeved bolero jacket
in humorless navy to be worn with a plain white shirt.
Hearing the price, Mom shook her head and said,
I can make that. And so she did and I the only one
who knew wishing, as always, for a family with funds
to afford ready-made.

A note from the school. Report to Homeroom 107.
Tall, patrician Sister Joan Patricia in elegant black-and-white
habit presided over two dozen assorted classmates—short,
thin, chubby, plain, pretty, noisy, silent—one more interesting
than the next. And so it was. Four years of studying
this one's platinum page-boy over her brilliant brains;
that one's plucked eyebrows above pale green eyes;
a confident redhead with free-range talent;
a simmering sexpot; Mary Jo's turquoise Chevy
and a best friend who would prove otherwise
when she stole my first boyfriend.

School has long been out.
Dominican High razed for a housing project.
Detroit itself, spooky as death.
September though still arrives whistling
with possibility.
What fresh books?
What new course?
Who and what are next?

Mom Said

Undershirts keep you warm.
Jeans make you rough.
Ice cubes freeze your stomach.
Shredded wheat scratches it.
Coke rots it.
Ginger cures it.
You don't need dessert.
Or a restaurant.
Work in the garden.
There are interesting articles
in the newspaper.
Smoking and drinking are bad.
Doctors don't know.
Wear navy, not black.
(Sorry)
Hell and Damn lead to worse.
(Sorry)
Clean house on Friday
then bake a cheesecake
or chocolate chip cookies.
While you iron, you can press
your troubles into the wrinkles.
Turn off the TV.
Take off your bra at five o'clock.
Soak in a tub at the end of the day.
You will worry about your children
for the rest of your life.

Working Girl

I was fifteen the summer I was summoned
out of a novel into Sammy's Market where Daddy
had the butcher concession.
The owner, a sad-eyed Greek, gave me a taste
of a mysterious salad with olive oil, oregano
and feta cheese.
I was given what passed for a company car:
a $300 considerably abused blue Plymouth to get to
and from the liver (beef or calf?), lamb chops (loin or rib?),
chicken (stewing or fryer?), kielbasa (smoked or fresh?)
and hamburger (chuck or regular?).

There were wooden slats on the floor, a long case
filled with red and pink animal parts, two scales,
knives, cleavers, a dangerous slicing machine and roll
of sturdy paper. You tore some off, placed the item
diagonally, bacon, say—63 cents a pound—and wrapped it
leaving a corner to tally the costs.
Daddy's brain was a computer that could add long sums
four across at a glance. My addition was cause for concern.
Because of that perhaps, some customers wanted only
my father with his stained white apron and twinkly greeting:
How's the prettiest girl in town?

A pair of saloon-like swinging doors led to the back
with saw-dusted floor, butcher block, deep sink, gas burners
where someone boiled wieners for lunch, and a restroom
you got in and out of fast. Behind a hefty door with heavy latch
was the freezing cold cooler hung with a side or two of dead cow
awaiting dismemberment.
And you wonder why I'm vegetarian.

The year was 1951. A stamp cost three cents;
gas was twenty cents. And the big clock in the store
took its sweet old time ticking away the two years it took
for me to make my getaway.

Late Breakfast

We were college freshman, Annette and I.
Not away in some swell dorm like you
but living at home and studying two nights a week
at her house; it was quiet there.
Mother sewing in her room, father out policing.
We were unlikely partners.
Annette, serious and focused;
I, yearning to concentrate yet doomed
to distraction with unrequited passion
ever checking for the hallowed hour
when the martinet called it a night.
At last, into the interrogation-bright
white kitchen for the holy ceremony.
Strips of bacon sizzling crisp.
Eggs slipped in sunny side.
Strawberry jam on Wonder toast.
Then perfection, unhappy without a flaw,
the police, off duty.
Stern, silent, scary as his work.
Didn't he just have to sit there
with his newspaper and his beer.

University of Tim Sullivan

An unsuspecting September morning
freshman year, day one. Perched near the top
of the lecture hall, I look down and see him, Tim.
And I am gone. Hopeless. Hapless. Sunk and snared
in an instant by the lean stride, wavy sandy hair,
and what I would come to know as teasing humor
in those eyes of blue mischief.
My major and minor declared—*T. S., I Love You*—
I proceed to shadow and stalk, register for his classes,
share his locker, drive him home, make him laugh,
and wait for the date that never comes.
You're too sophisticated for him, someone says.
Whatever that means, I vow not to be it anymore.
But nothing would unseat Tim from the cells of my soul.
Not quitting school for Advertising, not leaving for New York,
not marrying, mothering or moving back to the midwest.
Tim was aboard for the forty years it took for him
to be divorced, me to be widowed, and to realize,
over that long-awaited date, that I was too sophisticated
for the now grey-haired enthusiastic imbiber and father
of five who had grown up to be a dead ringer
for the world's worst president.

Mrs. Ferguson's
Residence for Women

The northeast corner of Madison Avenue and 68th street,
home to Max Mara, was once a sober abode for women
while they figured out their New York lives. I was there
via Nancy Rosen, a model and sister of the married
copywriter I had been typing for and trying to break up
with in what was then called the motor city. Nancy introduced
me to the importance of eye make up and to the glory
of a toasted buttered English muffin after a movie.

My third-floor window faced diagonally west
toward Central Park and south down Madison.
Phoebe's Whamburger occupied the half-basement
and was given to the occasional middle-of-the-night fire
that routed us into the street; Nancy clutching her fur,
thin old Mrs. Barrows huddled into her thin old robe,
Sophie, the zaftig opera singer from Palo Alto, the spinstery
WASP, Louise, from Lexington, Mass., Leah from Athens,
related to the shipping Greeks, and me, memorizing the scene.

I'd check Mrs. Ferguson's foyer after work, annoyingly anxious
for missives from the philandering copywriter.
Spying his envelope, I'd read the pages over and over.
They were clever and naughty, filled with encouragement
and promises to see me.

After an austere dinner in the window-less dining room,
Louise invited a few of us to her room to sip Harvey's Bristol Cream,
listen to the heavenly Brandenburgs and smoke cigarettes.

The copywriter, in town on business, monkey and otherwise,
once invited his sister to join us for dinner. She breezed into
the restaurant showing off a new tan raincoat from Brooks Brothers.
There would never be another coat that perfect.
Nancy was seeing a man who lived across from the residence.
Spotting them sometimes from my window,
getting out of a taxi late, I pined away for that life.

My own road took me out of Mrs. Ferguson's
and into a furnished flat a few blocks east.
Then learning some years later that the philanderer
had died of drink at forty-three.

The Last Supper

The tableau so deeply etched,
a lifetime later the mere words
Greenwich Village bring back
the anonymous brownstone.
Cozy living room, glowing hearth.
Crock of paté, Scotch and Kents aplenty.
Candlelit buffet, arroz con pollo in a clay pot.
Chianti. Laughter. Mozart.
Life might have ended that night
quitting while ahead but the host said:
You've got to meet our friend, John.
He'll love you.

John, phoned in Riverdale, arrived.
And I loved his green MG.
And dinner the next night
at his high-ceilinged club.
And the filet he fixed the night after
that might have been the beginning
of ever after had there been more dining
than wining; had he not smashed the MG
and ever called again.

Two bedrooms, two baths,
two-hundred dollars.
Carl Schurz Park at the river.
Toddler Meredith in a swing,
me in a peacoat.
Café du Soir up the street.
D'Agostino's on the corner
stocks an exotic new ice cream:
Rum Raisin. Black Raspberry.
Häagen-Dazs.

November, nineteen-sixty-five.
The first urban black out.
Opening our doors as never before,
we chat with neighbors by candlelight.
The chic young woman next door,
a *vendeuse* for Mainbocher.
Rose, the sitter from Jamaica
who fed Meredith lamb chops and rice,
talks into the night of her children far away.

Madison Avenue. I write Clairol ads
for Kay Daly of the pink Chanel suit.
Lunch with Julius and Bob and Alan:
rare cheeseburgers, martinis, Tareytons.
Dinner parties out of the tiny kitchen
from the pages of *Gourmet*.
Osso Buco. Cassoulet.
Quiche. Mousse. Pouilly Fuisse.

Meredith at three runs away from home
down the long hall, not looking back.
Then screams when I leave her at Montessori
across from flags flying at the U.N..
Marty takes a job in third-world Chicago.
There is no Häagen-Dazs.

St. Lucia and St. Martin

We never did vacation
on those eponymous islands.
Never got to Africa, China,
Japan or New Zealand either.
I didn't campaign hard enough;
he worried about funds.
Where we traveled to and often
was London in the days when theater
cost five or was it ten pounds?
He was in it for the tweed, never tiring
of stopping into every small shop hunting
the infinitesimal thread that whispered
into the fabric of his soul.
Home again, Mark Shale fashioned the jackets
that joined the rest of his exacting Ivy League.
I, who no one has labeled shabby,
felt next to him shabby.

Foretelling of a Wicked Gypsy

You will successfully climb out
of the accidental family into which
you landed purely for the challenge
of climbing out.
    You will be shy then not.
You will marry but not happily ever after.
    You will bear two beautiful daughters.
    One with house and hound and husband.
    One with God and God-knows-what.
You will see Paris and the rest
but love best a quiet country nest.
    You will smoke then not.
    You will drink then not.
You will shatter two arms and one knee.
Not at the same time.
Three surgeries will scar your view.
    You will know white-hot sex
    with a duplicitous snake.
You will meet a tall light stranger.
    And along this rough-hewn road,
    albeit strewn with occasional silk,
    you will empty your pen of all the sorrow
    and all the laughter of your soul.

Long Beach Long Ago

On summer Friday nights, Marty's parents' car and driver
ferried us from Manhattan to their Georgian house
on Long Island. Early the next morning we packed corned beef
sandwiches, rented a rowboat and fished for fluke
in Reynolds Channel. I, never able to hook a worm;
the sandwiches gone by ten o'clock. We'd come back,
clean our catch, then walk two blocks to the powdery beach
where I dreamed up ideas for the Maidenform campaign.

Evenings after drinks with Bertie's chopped liver in the sunroom,
the dour Nora served dinner on the patio. *Whatever you do,
don't ask how she is*, warned Bertie, *she'll say 'about the same.'*
I always forgot and she always said: *'about the same.'*
Thin bowls of chilled pink borscht were followed
by the freshly-cooked fluke and Nora's peach-plum pie.
Sunday mornings at the round oak table in the octagonal
breakfast room beneath a square yellow Tiffany shade,
there were bagels with Nova and sturgeon.

Jack, a martinet whose patients were the sole recipients
of his limited warmth, invariably rained on our parades.
With his unhappy wife, it was: *Easy on the bread, Bert.*
With me, it was a second Scotch. *That stuff's intoxicating.*
And cigarettes. *Those things are terrible for your circulation.*
Never mind that he was right.

Then, distracted by the glamour of all things New York
and ignoring the mismatch of our souls, there was a baby
to be named. Beginning with Amy and barely considering
the possibility of a son, we argued down the alphabet
for months, landing at last on Hillary. Which was not to be.
Looking into that miraculous face, I remembered a childhood
Meredith and that she is. Jack complained that she was named
for James Meredith. Another skirmish over naming another
daughter Daphne; Jack grousing that his patient, Daphne,
woke him at all hours.

On a morning when he and Bertie were visiting in what she
infuriatingly referred to as *your Chicago,* the phone rang
with news that Soc (Socrates), who had driven us to and fro
in Jack's Cadillac, had fallen asleep smoking and burned down
half the house that Jack built for his bride.
Bertie put it together again.

They and Marty are gone.
And all the nights of too many drinks and pointless regret,
of formless wishing for different and yearning for better,
all that has faded along with every other scene
from a bittersweet film called Long Ago.

Bertie

Not wanting to go to a party and have to smile
at people she didn't care to smile at, Bertie said:
*Just put my dress on a hanger and wave it
around the room.* My mother-in-law, the eternally
disappointed bride of the icy humorless Jack.
Whip smart and sassy. Faced with the prospect
of her handsome prince of a son marrying me,
the impoverished shiksa, she said, not joking:
Can't you two just have a long affair?
A woman of unerring taste, she found the perfect
flowers to ring the patio (salmon geraniums,
periwinkle ageratum) and never varied.
Perfection needed no perfecting.

Anyone can shop at Saks, she said, not adding
that it took a keen knowing to find the best things
for less. She spent her life prowling Loehmann's
for designer looks for next to nothing and dusty thrift
shops for treasure, chatting up everyone who came her way.
Home again, her sturdy blond curls tamped down in a chiffon
scarf, she puffed but didn't inhale a Pall Mall as she polished
the latest antique and spun her ongoing observations
on this one and that, but mostly about Jack and his
no end of shortcomings.

You should write a book, she said, implying I had the words
and she was rich material. Well, I did, Bertie. Wrote three,
in fact. And yes, you're in them. And still in my life.
I keep quoting you. Oh and remember wanting us to take
the painting of the boys and I said we had no room?
We did, of course, but I chose a poor time to be bratty.
And haven't stopped regretting it.

My Mother-in-Law, Myself

I've had my fun with it, Bertie said,
as to why she wasn't wearing
her whopping diamond anymore.
Really? You get to the stage
where you've worn enough jewelry?
It wasn't long before this once-passionate
collector of collectibles arrived with a fine
blue-and-white Spode tureen.
Carefully wrapped in a beach towel,
she hand-carried it from her Long Island
dining room to ours in Chicago.
Next came the cut-crystal punch bowl,
Florentine marble bust and Belgian painting.
Thirty years later, I am shipping a pair
of massive antique candlesticks to Meredith
in Colorado having already sent the Indian art,
Bokhara rug and Chelsea ship's clock.

The awful, no-place-to-hide truth is, it's time
some of the treasures we treasured moved on;
I've had my fun with them. But how did the years
of accumulating wind down so fast?
And at what point did I become my mother-in-law?

A Pink Salute

The year was winding down.
Marty was somehow still going
to the office although I dropped him off
an hour later and picked him up an hour earlier.
The doctor was impressed with his grit
but my own spirit was wavering.
It had been a long siege.
Driving home one morning, frightened
with gloomy thoughts of his looming death,
stopped at a light, I was shaken from my reverie
by something waving in the window ahead:
the pale pink of a baby's hand.
The cheer in that gesture.
The hand went down. We stopped again;
the hand shot up in a fist, opened, waved slowly
then disappeared. Oh, for one more look
at that fistful of life. The light turned green
and as I turned left, the tiny hand rose,
curled and waving.

Know that Stevie Smith poem:
Not Waving but Drowning?
This was not drowning.
This was an angelic salute waving
me to the finish line. *You can do it.*

Killing a Cockroach and
Feeling Plenty Good About it

The morning after Marty died
I awoke to hear his romantic voice:
I Concentrate On You.
It was one of his favorite ballads.
He was singing me into strength.

That first morning of my new life,
perched on the edge of the tub,
long antennae waving,
a large shiny cockroach
was all but trumpeting:
This is a test.
In the fifteen years we had lived there,
I had never seen one before.

I considered shrieking for my brother-in-law
then grabbed a shoe.
If this chapter was about survival,
I was ready.

While You Were Out
2010 Update to My Late Husband

The strange-as-fiction continues
since you left us sixteen years ago.
9/11 trumped Pearl Harbor
and we were ambushed into another war.
Everything's zipping,
zapping and morphing.
There are electronic cigarettes
and a pain named Palin.
Newspapers are on life-support.
We need a faster word than fast.
Virtually everyone's cyber-hyper.
Twittering. Rhymes with frittering.
Blogging. Rhymes with flogging.
Texting. While driving.
YouTubing.
Emailing.
Facebooking.
iPhoning.
iPading.
It's official:
Unable to live unconnected,
we are reaching out
and touching everyone
every second.
I, ever the Luddite,
am hiding under the covers
of Dickens and Dickinson
yet reading on a Kindle.
(You'd have to be here.)
As for leading, remember they said
we'd never elect a Catholic
and forget about a Jew or a black
in the—White House?
Hold the Jew for the moment
but *Ohbama.*
Uber smart.
(But it's the economy...)
And poetry-friendly.

Wall Street had the mother
and father of a meltdown.
No need to work at Marshall Field,
not that there is a Marshall Field,
but everyone is sobered up
and spending down.
You too would be pulling in
your Brooks Brothers belts.

It won't be give us this day
our Daley mayor anymore.
Governors all over the map
have self-destructed including
another of our own appalling pariahs.
A man named Madoff made off with mucho
and traded his penthouse for the pen.
What happened in Vegas didn't stay there
so O. J. too is in the slammer.
The Cubs are where you left them
more or less, mostly less.
I'm into meditation.
No not *medication*. Meditation.
I'm actually a tad more serene
except when I'm not.
Too many people we know
are dead, dying or old.
As for yours truly,
don't leave the light on.
I have many miles to write
before I sleep.

Adtopsy

Marion Dawson's obituary, he of the ad old days,
noted that he had written Rusty Jones's:
Rattle-rattle-thunder-clatter-boom-boom-boom.
They won't be listing my deathless lines
because the best were never to be.

Why is it I'm always drawn to your work? the CEO asked.
Would that he had been the decider or that I had learned
to sell my work or that my timing had been timelier.

I was twenty at BBDO-NY when my line for FTD fizzled:
Flowers. The shortest distance between two hearts.

Long before the greening of America, I created Green,
a lonely hearts editor for a dressing campaign:
How Green Was My Salad. How deep was my chagrin.

Two years before Pepsi coined it, I wrote:
The Schenley Generation. To general silence.

I Dreamed I was Well-Endowed in my Maidenform bra
captioned the sapphire'd siren in sables stepping into a Rolls.
The Agency was amused; the client never saw it.

Color Fatigue? Pour yourself a new head of hair.
A splashy Clairol spread that actually, if briefly, ran.

It's Betty Crocker, glad you liked it.
Commercials were shot, music recorded.
All was in readiness for the air till the supreme honcho
scolded: *We're hard-nosed marketing men;
we don't sing about cakes.*
They later changed their tune.
With someone else's.

Night and day, Dial is the one.
Keeps you fresh beneath the moon and under the sun.
Day and night, over the hide of you...
We storyboarded a Fred & Ginger in misty mauve
and a Johnny Mathis in New York sang the song.
Brilliant, said Neil. *Not so,* said the board.
You can't desecrate an American classic!
Fast forward but not by much to United's
Rhapsody in Blue.

How to sell Sears shoppers more than hard goods?
How to say there are clothes and such?
Come see the softer side of Sears.
Another preemie, resurfaced at another agency.

Ditto *Sweeten up, America,* for Brach's candies.

Join the V-8 health club. It's the least that you can do.
We set the words to a march but this being pre-fitness,
Campbell allowed that the H word would bring
the company to ruin.

The Agency was pitching the Army account.
Join the army and solve your fashion problems forever.

Copywriters weren't kept on based on actually hitting
them out of the park or I'd have spent all those years
selling you a lot of novels at Stuart Brent's bookshop.

Snapshots

Once upon a moonlit night in Capri,
we sat with coffee on the terrace of the Hotel Serena.
A silvery-haired man nearby
was joined by a blond companion wearing
an ivory skirt and rose silk sweater.
Buona sera, she spoke softly
as she kissed him.
It was the discreet shade of rose
and the romance in her greeting
that linger unmarred by the future.

In London, we sat in second-row seats
to see Edward Fox in *The Old Masters.*
In the first row, themselves straight out
of a drawing room, a neatly dressed, very old,
very thin man and his equally elderly tiny wife.
Darling, she said, *I've tucked your mac under your seat.*
A lifetime of caring in those words.

Another autumn, a table away in the hushed
and golden-lit Albert's Bar, a Jeanne Moreau
exhaling confidence. Sometimes serious,
sometimes chatting; a knowing laugh.
Dark chignon. Heathery mauve knit jacket.
Necklace of crystal and pewter.
Her friend in black; thick greying hair.
The waiter presented their steak before slicing.
They ate arugula, drank red wine.
A portrait in amber in a town by the sea called Nice.

Italian Movie

On a chilly October night in a somber hotel
dining room in Florence, a couple came in and took
the table in front of and to the left of ours.
He, late fifties, thin, dark-haired in jeans and navy fleece;
she, heavier with shoulder-length streaky blonde hair;
brown trousers, shapeless grey cable cardigan.
J's back to them both.

The waiter came by; I heard American voices;
saw diamond rings on her French-manicured
left hand. As J and I were served our pastas,
my attention was drawn to the man holding his head,
shoulders shuddering. I thought for a moment he was
laughing then realized he was sobbing. His wife sat rigid,
lips compressed; eye swollen, devoid of makeup.

J, hearing no conversation, whispered:
I'm thinking there's been a fight. I nodded.
Riveted, I kept glancing at the silent couple
as the waiter brought them water and salads.
Do we relinquish our rights to privacy in public?
Fair game for whoever wants in on our drama?
I had long been fascinated by the parade
and was given to staring. Had a parent died?
Had they lost a child? But they appeared
disconnected. And why did she seem angry?
Had they come to Florence for healing?

Cappuccino? J asked, bringing me back.
I'd better not. I had been sleeping poorly
and wasn't chancing not being served decaf.
The waiter removed their half-eaten salads;
served trout to him; linguine alle vongele to her.
Life limps along but not on an empty stomach.

J paid the check and pushed back his chair.
Let's get out of here.
The husband signaled for his bill.
No, I whispered, *I want to see them leave.*
He moved the check toward the candle,
not so broken as to just hand over a credit card.
Misery or no, we mind our truest selves.

There was no talking, no touching as they left,
although he held open the door.
We followed and I summarized the scene.
So what do you think?
They're breaking up.
Oh God! Of course! He's been having an affair,
she found out, and they came to Florence—
I bet they were here on their honeymoon—
to patch things up. And she just said No.

There was a price for spying; there would be little sleep
that night. The mute couple sat indelibly, actors
in a bleak, one-act play; I their hapless audience
compelled to witness their anguish.
I would remember her opening the gold-trimmed brown
handbag, looking for lipstick perhaps, zipping it closed.
I would recall her worn sweater, his half-turned collar.
But mostly, I would learn by heart their grief.
We are indeed our siblings' keepers. Enhanced
by their triumphs, diminished by their losses.

Frankenstein

Beneath the crossword puzzles, mystery novels
and mellow manner of this sweetheart of a fellow
lie the seamed and stitched innards of a creature
Mary Shelley might have conjured.

One night you're at Coco Pazzo laughing at his quips,
next you're in an ICU where he's attached to beeping
and buzzing machinery after life-and-death surgery
for a ghastly cancer and you figure this isn't anyone
you'll be having dinner with again.

But back he bounces and you're in London, Paris
and Longboat Key and then you're in an ICU
where he's just had a nick-of-time quintet of bypasses
and you look at all the tubes and dripping bags of never mind
and think: being single isn't the worst thing.

But here he is cracking wise again and there you are
in Florence, Venice and Dublin and then he's doubled over
with a double hernia in Sarasota. But he's back
and you're in Barcelona and then—what's that?
That is a retina of the detached variety and just when
he's about to move so he can't help.

But then he's all comfy in his cozy new digs
so you put your feet up and then you put them down
and run to St. Joe's for an emergency operation
for something unattractive that happens
after too many abominable abdominal procedures.
Wait. Why is that leg all red and bumpy?
Cellulitis? IV's? 14 pills for $1,000?

Well, all's well now. Which is where you came in
and where he is, is tucked in with the *Times* puzzle.
And I, having caught the bouquet of *je ne sais quoi*,
am the bride, so to speak, of Frankenstein.

Death Sentences

It happens poetically. Seventeen years to the day
of Marty's diagnosis, the giant Indian internist looks
at his notes and says: *Elevated liver chemistries.*
I'm scheduling you for an ultrasound tomorrow.
Could be hepatitis or cirrhosis.

    Cirrhosis? But I haven't had a drink in twenty-eight years.
Oh it can show up thirty-forty years later.

How is it my seemingly benign body
is staging a mutiny?
I check with Dr. Google:
Cirrhosis (scarring of the liver) can occur in a woman
who drinks 2-3 drinks a day for a decade.
I drank for two decades.
And smoked my fool head off.
And ate a cattle car of rare steak.
Life was a party, no?
Oh God. Imagine telling the girls.
And Jim. Who'll take care of him?
(Widows bearing briskets.)
There is no cure.
There is fatigue, bloating and death.
The upside: I won't have the Dow Jones
to worry about anymore. Or my blurry eye.
There is no sleeping. Not that I sleep on nights
when I'm not dying in the foreseeable.
But I love my life!
And I want to see Daphne married.
The kindly woman with the clipboard asks my date
of birth. *You don't look it. What's your secret?*
She's being nice. She knows.
What about all the laughing?
Isn't laughter life-enhancing?
I sign the form for the test:
liver, pancreas and kidney.
He never said all those things!

The pancreas is what did Marty in.
Irma, in her last months, bought cashmere.
I want to buy only time.
The darkened room is freezing, the technician wraps
my feet in warm blankets, has me turn this way
and that, hold my breath again and again.
I watch her watching the monitor, frowning,
pressing her lips together. Is that what she does
when she sees trouble?
But I have so many poems to write.
And no interest in seeing the dearly departed.
And what about the palm reader who saw a long life-line?

The next morning, a missed call from the doctor's office.
No message. Must be bad.
I call and leave a message.
Nobody calls back.
I read an article in the *Times:*
You're ill. What do you tell people?
I take a walk. Then decide to drive down there
and scream for attention.
But I'm hungry. Best not do that hungry.
I gulp a bowl of last night's Ribollita.
The phone rings.
Everything's fine. Your test is normal.
Nothing to worry about.
Except my eye.
And Daphne.
And Dow Jones.

Dead Kennedy

Two hours on the sofa
watching the widow in pearls
not weeping.
Barack and Michelle,
she behind a big black bow.
Clintons. Carters.
Bidens. Bushes.
Kennedy clusters
of princes and princesses
of privilege and infamy.
I know this clan.
Know their scrapes
and scraps of story.
Had noted all things Jackie.
Have breathed their very air
on the Cape.
This, another ceremony of loss,
shone bright light
into what made Teddy Teddy.
The power of steely persistence:
I can handle this.
The glory of re-birth.
The honor of service.
The kindness.
The humor.
A two-hour class:
Lessons from a master.

Cosmos

Cosmos brought out the gooey
in me. *Sweet Baby Darling,* I called him.
He liked that. And he liked listening
to a Shakespeare sonnet while we walked
in the park. He was a modest fellow
considering how beautiful he was.
How sweetly adorable.
He was just doing his job—loving us.
And being loved.
How blessed were we. How heaped with joy,
the gift of this heaven-sent soul.
Heaven. That's the key here.
God held out as long as He could.
Just had to have Cosmos back.
Anyone could see why.

(for Chris's beloved beagle)

Requiem for a Long Lustrous Life

How many helpings of raspberry mousse?
Chocolate soufflé? Cups of decaf?
How many Sunday lunches in New York?
Celebrations in Chicago with friends
and family, some now gone, at the harvest table
with black-and-white Wedgwood
and English silver I bought as a bride?
How many funny stories and bits of gossip
before the dinner that ended with cappuccino
ice cream and saw the silver spoon slip into the bowel
of the disposal that screamed its indigestion
and mangled the monogrammed treasure
of lo those many memories?

You Again

I saw you last night
pretending not to see me
pretending not to see you.
You, looking older;
my heart, mended
from the blender
you put it through.
Fancy you passing
for just another art lover
at just another opening
in your who me? navy suit
and striped shirt.
There was no mistaking
that trademark way you cup
your hand to make a point.
But you, with a gold band?
Monogamous? No.
You've merely upped the ante.
Conning the missus must take
ever more cunning for ever more
illicit thrills.

It was only a matter of when
and where you'd turn up,
this being a big small town.
I had been looking for you
every day in the obituaries.
Remember how we read them
for the secrets of success?
Hope of your demise, however,
is hopeless; you appear
to be hideously healthy.
And, as only the good die young,
you've decades to lie before you sleep.
Not that you are entirely
without value. Seeing you
has produced this poem.
I won't be thanking you, though.
Not after you kept me up all night.

Life Begins the Day
You Start a Garden – *Chinese proverb*

My people were farmers in Poland.
In the new country, my mother and Ciocia,
our merry aunt and grandmother stand-in,
were gardeners. Mom, tending her felicitous
mix of iris or flags, as she called them,
and poppies, tiger lilies and a few roses,
none as showy as Ciocia's. *She has better soil,*
Mom said, attempting to hide her chagrin.

Planted early in my soul, these roots bided
their time till the little red house in the country
meant I too could fall to my knees and be happy.
Now I too was welcome in the nursery, inhaling
the greeny perfume of geranium; plotting this tulip,
that daffodil. Trying the inky diva, Delphinium;
my digs not grand enough. Trying the hollyhock
that sprang perennially behind Mom's garage
but not beside my fence. Rosy coneflowers
though never stopped showing up and lilac
stretching for sun and pale iris and peonies;
their offshoots still gracing Tina's, Nancy's
and Judy's places.

The little red house is no more.
Time will come and steal your love away,
Shakespeare wrote. So we arise, dream anew
and nurture blossoms twenty-five stories in the sky.
Moonflowers and morning glories on willow branches.
Monarch butterflies on periwinkle scaevola.
A cardinal vine with whirling hummingbird.
An arbor wreathed in scented white clematis.
Emerson said: *The earth laughs in flowers.*

Silversea.
Ship of Caribbean splendor
and sometimes seasick sailing.
St. Thomas. Port of fall.
Ambulance.
X-rays.
Orthopod.
Left arm; fractured radius.
Right knee cap, in pieces.
A symmetry.
Back story:
2005. Lyon. Port of fall on face.
From this trip forward,
you and your mates
may cruise to amuse.
I, on the other hand, foot and femur,
must choose to refuse.

Question

You who arm your cool
with hearts and arrows,
skulls and bones,
and snakes and anchors—
who think to ink your flesh
with vines and designs entwined
with demons and dragons,
I Love You Mom and Semper Fi—
any thoughts about
how those tattoos will play,
say, in the Home?

Trust Me

Somebody asked Woody Allen:
What do you hope they'll say
when you're dead?
    I think he's still breathing.

I care nothing about commentary
after the fact. What I wish they were
saying here-and-now is:
    What does she do with those billions?

Ah, the comfort of having enough
not to worry about having enough.
To nestle within the cozy folds
of a trust fund impervious to the jitters
of Wall Street.
To ponder matters loftier than:
Will it run out before I run down?
Imagine spending the energy I squander
on fear on well, you, for instance.
Even now, I could be opening
the Bill Gates to your checkbook.
It would be lovely. Trust me.

Bag Lady

We are no longer slaves to skirt lengths
yet the tyranny of fashion continues
and nowhere more graphically
than in the handbag department.
Those garish Guccis and showy Chanels
swaggering toward the six figures.
Are they not the empress's new totes?
Mea culprit. I fell for a Birkin by an Hermés
defector who black-markets the impostors
for a sliver of the sticker price.
The down side: heavy as bricks, it is a drag
to drag around.
So, having bagged the albatross, I, who once
did time in Advertising so I could stockpile
Sonia Rykiels, have taken refuge in a find from Filene's.
It weighs as lightly on me as it did my credit card.
Thus, to the world of must-see-and-be-seen-in
symbols of status, I say, bah humbag.

L.A.

See the woman listing to the left?
That's me, en route to a meeting
of Listaholics Anonymous.
I'm up for charter membership.
Step One:
Consider the consequences
of not making all those calls.
Surely every last one of you
will not wilt for lack of my chatter.
As for the To Do list I carry in my bag,
some of those items:
  • car mats from Pep Boys
  • a new sewing box
  • contact cement *(for what?)*
have languished undone since the 1900s.
Netflix lingered on a list till I joined at last
and now have sixty films to view but when?
given I am given to:
  • a long line of books to read
  • a long walk to take
  • a long list of people to invite to a party
    we will never give because we like friends
    in 2's and 4's but not 44's.
Step Two:
Toss the whole lot of them. *Be listless.*
Clear the desk and, thus, the mind.
Face the day minus columns of names
and numbers and a fat black marker to obliterate
the over-and-done-with.

Sounds simple but the lust for lists dates
from the primordial ooze.
Surely, Napoleon crossed off countries to conquer.
Gandhi kept track of his mantras.
And once upon a world, the Almighty
chiseled in stone:
- create a garden
- add a snake
- come up with ten shall-and-shall-nots.
Today, His BlackBerry would read:
- whip up a hurricane
- let it snow
- paint a sunset

What's Happening

Used to be I couldn't see the wrinkles
without glasses. Didn't hear a chorus
of crickets in my ears. Didn't feel this ache
and wonder about that pain.
What's happening is that everyone else's narration
of woes *du jour* now includes mine.
I, who once skipped between, not landed on,
landmines.
Not complaining, just reporting a macular hole
in my retina. The requisite gas bubble required
keeping my head down for nine days.
Time, for once, didn't fly, and the surgery
for the cataract that followed was followed
by chronic swelling that produced a shadow.
Dr. Google diagnosed: detached retina.
I denied that. But that it was.
And a second gas bubble meant seven more days
memorizing the pattern in the rose rug.

Not complaining, just reporting.
It's getting darker.
The wind is picking up.
There appear to be fewer life rafts.

Rave Review

The toddler wheeling toward me,
eyes ablaze, face aglow, hugely grinning,
was clapping his chubby hands, applauding
everything and everyone in sight.
I thought to ask his mother about
her happy little chap. In a rush though,
I raced on, smiling, my spirit sparked.

We worry at all the ways the world
has spun awry, but let it be known that,
once upon a blue summer's day,
one young viewer gave the whole shebang
a sitting ovation.

symptom
second opinion
broke her hip
degenerative
broke his shoulder
biopsy
third opinion
quintuple bypass
M.R.I.
surgery
they got all of it
I.C.U.
stenosis
rehab
spondylolisthesis
epidural
c.t.scan
angiogram
shouldn't be driving
on a walker
assisted living
D.N.R.
I always liked him

Remember Pay Phones?

Metal cabinets.
Slots for coins.
Heavy black receivers.
Steel cords.
They once cost a nickel.
Then a dime.
Then a quarter.
Then two quarters.
If you were long-winded
a non-negotiable voice demanded
another dime to continue.
They're disappearing, those artifacts,
headed to the landfill or wherever
your old Walkman, VCR and Polaroid
have gone to their rest.
The lonely remaining few are fading
phantoms of another era,
echoes of another dialogue.

Is that your cell?
Tomorrow you won't remember
cell phones.

Ghost Stories

What is this if not a rehearsal for the next chapter,
this keen hearing of each tick of the clock?
Seventy is after all not fifty.
Seventy swoops in and sweeps you into the room
that may well be the penultimate.
Meanwhile, those who have left the stage waft back
wanting not to be forgotten for their parts.

The long-gone husband; the echoing jokes still funny,
the occasional sighting of his particular plaids.
He spirits back to sing the Messiah. Tina spotted him
in Detroit, I in a Florida church; white beard ever trim,
tenor-ing his Jewish heart out welcoming Jesus.

Irma, in her 54th Street duplex, smoking and sipping
Muscadet in the lemon slipper chair; I on the chintz sofa,
telling tales before lunch at *Le Bec Fin*.

Brilliant beautiful Judy, my cubicle-mate at BBDO on Madison.
Pal to Sinatra, Warhol, et al; her celebrated, brazen mouth
silenced at sixty-two.

Barbara, a latter-day Job. All but impervious
to the horrors that life never stopped hurling at her.
Death must have seemed like a cruise.

Joan, the laser that paused then passed in the night.
I knew her too little too late.

Yes, you there in the mists, I am inching nearer.
Don't rush me.

The Holy Goal

Why are we here?
What makes us tick?
What bright carrot
jiggles our stick?
Climbing Kilimanjaro
and curing cancer.
Is that the answer?
Losing ten pounds
and finding true love?
Winning the Lottery?
Putting for par?
Out-writing Bellow
for a Nobellow?
Nixing war
and fixing peace?
Nah.
We just wanna be on *Oprah*.

Practice Dying, Plato Said

Forget practice.
Say I'm gone.
If not today,
tomorrow.
Don't let them be sad.
Or let them be sad
and be done with it.
Tempus fugit.
But imagine their dealing
with the detritus.
Good Lord, she kept this?

I try to throw something
away every day
yet stuff sticks like Velcro.
Problem being,
ghosts of regret haunt
things long gone.
Will the next to go
leave a new hole in my heart?
If it does, does it matter?
Does matter matter?
If I'm dead?
Not if. When.
When I'm dead.
When?

Weather Report

Art Buchwald said that when he was a kid,
there was none of this wind-chill business.
It was cold, very cold, or it was freezing.
In my youth, there weren't any June-in-December
or November-in-May days either.
May was simply the softest, sweetest month.
School was almost over. You got out your shorts
and tee shirts—plain ones, no graphic graphics,
and red sandals and you played Monopoly,
rode your bike, listened to *Let's Pretend*
and slept in shortie pajamas in a room
that on hot sticky nights, if you were lucky,
had a fan.

In other words, things are different today.
Well, yes and no. Know how you read about
some outrageous unraveling of the culture
only to learn that it happened a hundred years ago?
Trouble is, we're writing new chapters
of those stories and a hundred years from now,
assuming there is a hundred years from now,
they'll be reading about our SUV's and PCP's,
global boiling, never mind warming, carpal tunnels
and cancers and kids killing kids on a screen
instead of striking them out on a field;
comics grossing gazillions being gross
and how the U.S. of A., once the proudly-we-hailed
good guys in white hats were ambushed into black.

I don't know. Is it me or do you feel a draught?
What I do know is, until someone shows up
to turn this thing around,
we need to get our affairs in order.

Plan B

Our elders in their elder years,
their long days work done,
rocked golden in their easy chairs,
nest eggs intact, all of it over
often by three-score and ten.
Not so we, tread-milling into our nineties
packing cancers and shriveled savings.
We had been sticking around
to do more, see more;
have Visa, will buy more.
But with the movie of fantasy faded
to black-and-white reality, what now?
More denim, less designer.
Think Goodwill not Gucci.
More nesting, less jetting.
More casseroles, less cocaine.
Curling up in old jeans
with macaroni and cheese
and a Christie mystery
may be just the cure
for the uncommon depression.

Now Voyager Not

What happened?
Where is the I who lived to roam
London,
Lisbon
and Rome?
Bound for Barbados,
Bermuda,
Barcelona,
Dublin
and Athens?
What happened?
The husband who needed prodding
to pack for Paris,
Portofino
and Prague packed for the yonder beyond.
The sweetheart needs no prodding.
But I am now the I who,
rather than nipping to Nantucket,
Antigua
and Jerusalem,
finds travel a travail.
Who discovers new cities of splendor
re-arranging the twigs in her nest.

To you who yet yearn for the tumult
as you fasten your seatbelt
and zoom to anonymous rooms;
who log ever more sights and delights,
hurtling home to book still another,
I wish a *tres bon voyage*.
And please close the door softly behind you.

B.C.

Before cellphoning.
Before computing.
Before communicating
ran amok and hooked us
online and sunk us
in a ceaseless peace-less
parade of palaver,
there was stillness.

The *Times* told of a man
who spent Sundays
speaking not a thing to not a soul.
A variation presented itself
like a present to me:
to salvage the remaining shred
of peace and quiet
(not that it's been peace or quiet
since about 4th grade, still)
I have vowed to keep my Sundays
Mac-free.
A small step yet giant,
for without email or bills,
with nary a glimmer of Google
or even a needy poem to reel me in,
I roam the soundless corridors
of my mind
and confront the silence.

Entropy

Never did like that word:
a process of running down to chaos.
It all heads there:
the car, the computer,
the windows, the dryer.
So you nip here, tuck there,
and mind your inventory
of duct tape and people to talk to nicely
to better your chances
they'll come fix whatever
just came off its hinge
not necessarily excluding you.
Except that they will tend to you
only till they're tending their own
escalating disarray.

Freud said the cornerstones
of humanity are Love and Work.
He might have added Repair.

Disappearance

If by no longer visible,
you wonder what happened
to the shiny brown bob I once swung.
If you miss the days
when we sweetly sang:
My Country 'tis of Thee.
If you remember the smell
of burning leaves.
Watching a ballgame
and not thinking:
performance enhancement.
Not knowing:
performance enhancement.
If you recall manners
and kindness
and quiet.
Musical music.
A million being a zillion.
Rapping meaning wrapping.
Tying a shoe without
sass from your back.
Thinking retirement meant
putting your feet up
on the old hassock and forgetting
to lock the door but nobody
broke in anyway.
If you wonder what you can count on.
What's in for the longest of hauls.
What appears to never disappear.
That would be fear.

The World According to Susie

Also known as: The Book of Knowledge.
You're in it, I'm in it, and so is everyone else
we know, don't know or may have heard of.
With all-seeing eyes in front, back and on top
of that beautiful curly head, Susie notes
our comings, goings and foolings around.
With her keen mind—actually a file cabinet
she picked up at Goodwill—she knows
what we've been up to or down with,
when we need to buy clothes, sell a condo,
see a doctor or teach our old jewels some new tricks
(wielding her welder, that dreary weary is now a wow pin).
All this amid tenderly tending her girls and grandkids
and 3rd-time's-a-charm-Irving *(How do you like his shirt? $2)*
and reminding you not to love anything that doesn't
love you back; how to travel from LBK to MA without luggage
and not to insure your diamonds because that's like
re-buying them. Then she's off to re-do the floors
and baths, paint the kitchen, put up art, take down doors,
and paste this bit of razzle to that piece of dazzle.
The world is, after all, Susie's easel.

Zippity-Sue-dah has time for everything
and everybody, including having a ball on the courts
but no time or need for lists; they're in her head.
Ask her how she is. *I'm divine,* says Susie
in that naughty, bawdy way. And is she ever.
You can have your Hillarys and Obamas.
I say *Think Fink For President.*
Listen. She'd have every last one of us
shaped up and home in time for dinner.

(for Susan Silver Fink)

Good Night

Please, someone, explain
why young women are wearing dresses
that look like nightgowns
or nightgowns that would be dresses
on the streets. Silky hems everywhere
are kissing the pavement.
To wit, a summer sighting at CVS:
A bosomy blonde in a floor-length
strapless number in shimmery shades
of pumpkin, gauzy as a ball gown,
buying toothpaste.

a) She was en route to her nuptials.
b) This is the ultimate day-into-night dressing.
c) The culture is out to delete me completely.

They're Out There

And yet another fashion
I'm the last to hear about.
When did open-air breasts
become the thing—the things—
to bare?
Bliss being ignorance
and this being summer,
hordes of the nubile
are semi-dressed in tight tops
with steep necklines,
the better to display their décolletage
on the street, in cafes,
on the bus—you name it,
you are witness to free-ranging bosoms.
Perhaps they have undergone
augmentation and seek approbation.
But did their mommies
never tell them mammaries
are a turn-on?
As in *asking for it?*

Waiting for Rubens

Not the sandwich, though that's not a bad idea.
I was thinking of a latter-day Peter Paul
who will make it fashionable again
to spill over with flesh and flab
and pounds of plenty, i.e, the Rubenesque babes
of bounty, lounging in the altogether having had
half a haunch at lunch, reaching for a peach
and counting conquests not calories.

Basta! It's time that thin isn't in, that more of us
to love is not to be scorned.
I have been dieting for fifty years and have had my fill
of supermarket cover girls, narrow as arrows.
Bring on the bacon cheeseburger, super-size fries
and hot fudge sundae. Hold the ice cream.

Chess

It's the Great Pumpkin
moving us hither and yon
like the sightless pawns we are
mucking about in the interminable
fog of not knowing.
Forever having to find new footing.
Praying for the power
to do this or to be that
in a game of Olympian skill
yet set with puny players
on a wobbly board
and thus ever flailing
and failing to hold on.

Night Life

According to a recent newspaper article,
while I am tucked in with my Kindle,
other women—decades younger, gorgeous
in their skimpy dresses, their dates having bribed
the doorman $20 to $500 for entry—
are arriving at midnight at a dimly-lit club
where the music (Top 40, eclectic, hip-hop,
pop and rock) is ear-blasting LOUD and thumping.
Some of these babes and beaux will hang
from the rafters and dance.
Some will drink $2,000 Cristol champagne;
some, $450 Dom Perignon or $275 Grey Goose.
Outside these venues, schlubby blokes
cool their uncool heels hoping for admission.
Inside, the well-heeled and DJaded
rockers and rebels are having fun
and losing control.
And what are *you* doing Friday night?

Having a Poem

Carl Sandburg said:
> *Telling a man to write a poem*
> *is like telling a pregnant woman*
> *to have a red-haired baby.*

Seven-year-old Sadie Heller said:
> *Writing a poem gets my brain moving.*

From where do they wing in,
these wisps that would be poems?
A sight, a site, a sound, a smell
and you're back in fourth grade
studying the flawless Dawn Okie.
Come play with me,
do the laundry later,
nudges the notion.
I'll hide; you seek.
You start there
I'll hie you here
behind this tree.
Not the willow weeping
over your mother's grave.
This one, with the woodpecker
going at it out on that limb.
Now you're in the garden.
(Why are tiger lilies spotted not striped?)
Now you're peering into
the cool green velvet moss
hunting elves and fairies.
You nearly saw one that once.
All right, you're fading, go.
Come back though.
Because you'll miss this bliss.
Go, gather more data, he warned.
You'll find what we have is very rare.
True, he was riddled with No.
I, though. am spilling with Yes.
I am the bells of Christmas.

Cinnamon toast in Owosso.
Flooring it to Ann Arbor.
I am Sharon's coral swing.
Audrey Angel's tomatoes.
Donna's new breasts.
That Phoebe Snow song.
Fred Astaire's shadow.
Mrs. Mowcher's umbrella.
Tim's at the door.
And Jam's old cat.

I will never stop meddling,
muttering and mattering.
Call me maddening.
At times, I am iambic.
I am poetry.

Old Woman Walking

Somewhere in a green park
an old woman is walking slowly
and talking to no one unless you count
the yellow lab off its leash
or that sorry fellow on the bench
or the nanny oblivious of the sun
in the baby's eye.
That's what happens at that age.
You talk to yourself.
But she could be continuing a last
conversation with her even older husband.
She might be reciting the recipe
for the chocolate cake her mother
always made with Crisco.
Maybe she's saying the sonnet
about not admitting impediments
between the marriage of true minds.
Or the one that compares her
to a summer's day.
Or the poem about being too busy
to stop for death.
Her head filled with a lunar beauty,
bits of rhythm and rhyme,
well-worn words stacked on shelves
that glow there waiting their turn
to be aired on the path in the park
of an autumn afternoon by a woman
no longer young.

Onward

You don't see Billy Collins sitting down
to write a novel. Or Kay Ryan. Ted Kooser.
Or Wisława Szymborska, for that matter.
Versifiers stick to their lasts, grateful
for the narrow brevity of their craft, knowing
that however many pages they penned wouldn't pack
anywhere near the comfort of a *Consolation,*
the touché of a *Revenant,*
the punchline of a *Four-Moon Planet,*
a mere three of Billy's beauties.
Nor is it likely any of their wordier works
would knock old Roth off his pedestal
or have a hapless reader up to all hours to find out how it ends.
Poets get to where they're going fast
and everyone else gets to go to sleep.

So why should I, who also show up in the vineyard,
be rattled by yet another agent's rejection
of yet another iteration of my fiction?
Because far from unflappable, my persona
is of the ragtag variety; I am given to flap.
There is hope, though. And that, Miss Dickinson,
no windbag herself said, is the thing with feathers.

Onward. Which happens to be the last word
of the last novel I shall ever write
and you will never read.

Would it Kill You
to Send Me a Grandchild?

The children of my friends, bless them,
reproduce incessantly and I dutifully send off
the hand-knit sweater or carefully selected books
along with my loving wishes.
I'm happy for them. Really.
My grandchild-free life abounds with the passion
and projects Betty Friedan said we need
for a meaningful maturity. However.
Last week, as I was sugaring my latte at Starbucks,
a woman my age, sugaring her latte,
said softly to the serious little toddler in her arms:
What will I do without you?
Which makes me wonder what I'm doing without you,
my angel baby, napping somewhere on a cloud,
unaware of all the candy you could be having
while we snuggle and I read *Skiddycock Pond*
for the hundredth time.

We Called it "The Country"

As in we'll be in the country this weekend,
a tony piece of the east I brought back
to boring old Chicago. If New Yorkers were off
to the Hamptons and Fire Island, the least
or the most I could do was make do.

Seventy-five miles north, the house was on the edge
of a ramshackle resort in Genoa City, Wisconsin.
In 1967, during the first of seasons that ran
from April to November, Marty began painting
the small ranch barn red; it took him four years.
The inside, meanwhile, was newly white with red doors,
the redwood furniture recovered in navy plaid.
A matching teddy bear sat near the hearth
and kept watch.

Driving up on Friday evenings, often in a violent storm,
Marty would squeeze one of our hands and say,
Isn't it great to be a family?
We'd stop for ice cream at Howard Johnson's
or Dairy Queen in Twin Lakes. Often closing,
they reopened in deference to my desperation.

On clear starry nights, the Big Dipper hung over
the chimney and after unpacking the denim Country Bag
(that continues to ride in my trunk) we fell asleep
on slightly clammy sheets to the crickets' castanets.

Being out of the city was bliss, and it began when we turned
off the highway onto the gently hilly road that by day
was a bucolic study in barns, farmhouses, blue skies,
waving rows of corn and black-and-white cows.
Leaving Grandma Moses on Sunday nights, my spirits slumped.

We worried about fresh trouble. There were occasional
plumbing problems or a baby mouse petrifying in a drawer;
a squirrel once munched a bedspread and baseboard.
Twice there were burglars. New linens and small TV
the first time; antiques and dinner forks, the second.

I posted a notice:

> Would-be Thieves:
> We have removed all valuables.
> There is no TV.
> No liquor.
> No money.
> No golf clubs.
> No reason to break into our little house.
> Ask God to forgive you for even thinking of stealing.

We lived thief-free ever after.

The property came with daylilies, iris, peonies and lilacs
that forever strained for sun. When the perennial border
turned shady, we hauled it all to a sunnier plot
visible from the kitchen window.

Friday nights, I took a flashlight to see what had bloomed
during the week and imagined the plants rousing themselves.
Wake up, she's here. There were magenta liatris,
purply monkshood, poppies, Shasta daisies, balloon flowers
and roses that didn't survive the mean winters. A rainbow
of hollyhocks dazzled one summer, disappeared the next.
We planted hundreds of tulips from Mary Black's in Deerfield:
showy parrots in greeny-orange, white and black;
red Queen of Shebas tinged with gold, and daffodils.
Daphne's tiny hand the right size for placing the bulbs
in holes painstakingly dug by Himself.
Come spring, we harvested buckets of blooms
that filled the car with their waxy fragrance.

We put in a long row of cotoneasters near the road
and added more trees, including an Emerald Queen maple
that grew majestically despite a mysterious gouge
and a Mountain Ash from Tina and Pete that didn't produce
its bittersweet berries until our last year.

We Called it "The Country"

Down the lane beside the corn farm, we gathered wildflowers
and black raspberries from prickly bushes and picked strawberries,
warm and luscious, at Vincent's farm. The girls sat on the truck,
waiting to be old enough to be trusted in the rows.

Mourning doves echoed my childhood. Elegant redheaded
woodpeckers hammered on hollow trees. Blue jays squawked
over whose turn it was in the birdbath.

Saturday mornings, I walked and wrote jingles while Marty
and the girls shopped at Sentry for killer-sweet Kringles.

We drove to Marino's in New Munster for pizza, pasta
and iceberg salad or had drinks across the road in Elaine
and Monroe's screened house. The wonderfully able Monroe
enabled us to be homeowners. *Marty was always saying,
'How do you turn this thing on'? Or 'How do you turn this thing off'?*
They often joined us for Chinese at the Golden Buddha
in a hayfield we couldn't find without them.

Sundays, on the way back, we stopped at the Kaplans'
or they or others would come up for barbecues; Marty grilling
flank steak, the kids husking corn from Klopstein's.

Afternoons, the girls sat on benches at the coffee table
bent over their beading. And caught fireflies at dusk.
What do you like best about the country? I asked
six-year-old Meredith. *Mother Nature.*
There was a birthday party and a poem that began:
*Who in the world is about to turn seven?
Is it Meredith Blinn? Oh my heaven...*

Marty and Meredith played golf, a passion that piqued
her at nine. The girls swam at the club and had English
riding lessons at April's. *Would you consider Meredith
joining the circuit? She's good enough.*
Sorry, Honey, we didn't.

There were naps on the screened porch built over Marty's
protest—*You keep spending like this, we'll never have enough
for retirement*—and from which he rarely budged.
Toward the end, I tried to read there but mostly stored
the green of the trees and speck of a barn two farms away,
knowing they wouldn't last.

We played Scrabble and Gardyloo, the dictionary game based
on made-up meanings that produced Daphne's show-stopping
definition of stennic: *Floyd Stennic, Wanda Stennic,
Beulah Stennic and Egbert Stennic—the whole Stennic family.*

There were annual Hat Pictures posted on the fridge;
the girls wearing floppy straw hats holding Pie,
the beloved dachshund and later, Mac, the mini hysteric.

We limped along with a single loo till I went over
Marty's head and added a grand new one.
I thought you said bathroom, not ballroom.

Nine miles away, Lake Geneva meant Ivy League shopping,
a bookstore, movies and a walk around the shore.
The lure in neighboring Richmond was Anderson's trove
of handmade filled chocolates. Milk or dark?

Loud acorns pounded the roof during howling storms;
lightning threatened the trees. The un-air conditioned
house was usually cool although there were a few steamers
every summer. One sticky night, a guest of Daphne's,
who lived in Winnetka splendor, woke us.
Mr. Blinn? Are you sure the air conditioning is on?
Yes, he said, with impressive authority. *Oh, okay.*
And the little princess padded back to bed.

And sharing it all with the Virginias and Tina, Pete and Peter,
who especially liked the night an alarming party of large lizards
slithered in from a two-day rain. And Valerie, who found every
allergen to sneeze at and who staked out a blanket away
from the fray, singing and planting the seeds of her future.

Then, as if we awoke from a dream, the idyll was over.

April 18, 1993.
What would have been Marty's sixty-third birthday
dawned sunny, cloudless and freezing.
It was Earth Day.
We scattered Marty's ashes beneath an ancient oak tree
in our woods, some too across the road at the Roths'
and tied one of his hundred ties, a brown-and-green rep,
onto a limb.

The girls moved away that summer.
The house wasn't home anymore.
That was clear the weekend a few friends
came up and didn't stop chattering.
They knew nothing of listening to crickets
and birdsong and keeping the silence.

After twenty-eight autumns, I closed the red door
for the last time, lay on the ground
and watered the grass with my tears.

For several years, I made the round trip
every fall to torment myself with memories
and check on the state of the tie.
It held on and held up remarkably
till the weather finally had its way.

All those long-ago scenes are stitched together
in a distant tableau:
Marty, loving and funny to the end.
Meredith and Daphne growing far too fast.
Family and friends laughing 'round the redwood table.
The scary night I heard something in the bushes
and Scott slept with a large knife to protect us.
I had to go to the bathroom, Daphne said,
but I was afraid Scott would kill me.
And floating over it all, the ephemeral rapture
of day after soft blue day.
The two most beautiful words, said Henry James,
are summer afternoon.

122

Acknowledgments

Warmest thanks to Arlene Wanetick for the weekend that launched the poems.

To Lorelei and Bruce Bendinger who launched the books.

And to the readers and listeners who keep me afloat.

About the Author

In a previous incarnation, Lucia Blinn was an advertising copywriter (see Adtopsy, page 42). Since skipping away from the business in the late eighties, Lucia has been scribbling poems and happily sharing them with various gatherings in Chicago and Sarasota.

luciablinn@gmail.com